# God's Armorbearer II
## How To Bloom Where God Has Planted You

*by*
*Terry Nance*

# God's Armorbearer II
## How To Bloom Where God Has Planted You

*by*
*Terry Nance*

**Harrison House, Inc.**
Tulsa, OK 74136

Unless otherwise indicated, all Scripture quotations are taken from the *King James Version* of the Bible. Other scriptures are from *The Amplified Bible* (AMP), 9th Ed. Copyright © 1965, 1972 by Zondervan Publishing House, Grand Rapids, Michigan.

*5th Printing*
*Over 52,500 in Print*

*God's Armorbearer II*
*How To Bloom Where God Has Planted You*
ISBN 0-89274-733-1
Copyright © 1994 by Terry Nance
Agape Church, Inc.
P.O. Box 22007
Little Rock, Arkansas 72221

Published by Harrison House, Inc.
P.O. Box 35035
Tulsa, OK 74136

# Dedication

I dedicate *God's Armorbearer II* to my dad, Tommy Nance, who taught me the importance of being on time, keeping my word, and staying with a job until it was finished. He has played an important part in my life and ministry.

Also, I extend special thanks to the Agape Church Staff who through their diligence and experience provided the keys used in this book.

# Contents

# Foreword

Several years ago, we were one of the host churches for the Billy Graham team when they came to town to prepare for a crusade in Little Rock.

I remember being introduced to the man who addressed our steering committee. He said that he was one of the youngest crusade directors on Dr. Graham's team. He had only been with the ministry twenty years.

Later, we hosted a meeting at our church, where Cliff Barrows spoke and George Beverly Shea sang. As we all sat in our guest room before the service, they began reminiscing and talking about the "forty-plus" years they had been with Billy Graham. It was so precious to hear them laugh as they remembered the funny things, and yet at the same time, it was powerful to hear of the faithfulness to their call.

In Paul's charge to Timothy, as he finished his course and kept the faith, he charged Timothy to be diligent in coming to him. Then he began to share about those who had forsaken him and had done him much evil: **Demas has forsaken me, having loved this present world . . . only Luke is with me. Take Mark and bring him with you: for he is profitable to me for the ministry** (2 Tim. 4:7-11).

At this writing, Terry Nance and I have been together fifteen years. I suppose Terry has done everything there is to do in the growth of a church. He always was faithful to "bloom where he was planted." The Bible says a faithful man will abound in blessings. He is fulfilling his calling in this ministry and is a blessing to the world through our Agape School of World Evangelism, of which he is the dean of students. Terry and his wife, Kim, are two of the finest people we have ever known, and I know his second book on the ministry of an armorbearer will impart a spirit of excellence to your life.

Happy Caldwell
Pastor, Agape Church
Little Rock, Arkansas

# 1

# The Hour of the Local Church

From the prophetic signs happening every day, it seems Jesus is soon to return. That is why I feel such an urgency about each member of the Body of Christ finding his place and remaining faithful, so we can be productive in God's Kingdom. I believe this is the hour of the local church.

The local church is the *hub* from which all ministry gifts are to function and the center out of which they are to flow. In the local church, you find what is needed to build the character of Christ in us. Each member of the Body of Christ should discover his or her gift and calling, and then become fully connected to a local church, submitting one to another and submitting to the God-called pastors and leaders there.

When people come into my office desiring to become part of our local church body, my first question always is, "What church do you come from, and who was your pastor?"

You can tell what type of Christian you are dealing with by the answer you get. Millions of Christians attend church services only on Sunday mornings and are not committed physically or spiritually to that church. Their reasons for attending range from tradition to religious duty to social acceptance in the community. Going to church once a week eases their consciences of religious obligations.

Think what could happen in this country if those people would get on fire for God and begin to release their gifts and talents in the Body! We would see the world reached with the Gospel. The local church is called to touch

11

its community, town, or city for God. To the reader, I would ask these questions:

- What part are you to play?

- Where can you get involved?

- What resources do you have available?

- What opportunities lie before you?

- What do the leaders of your local church need from you?

- How many times have they asked for help, or how many times have you volunteered?

Take a look at what you have to offer your local church. You may feel that you have nothing to offer, but that is never true of anyone. Each born-again believer has something to offer that is unique. Each Christian has a call on his life which will become apparent once he is involved in a church.

First Peter 4:10 (AMP) says:

> **As each of you has received a gift (a particular spiritual talent, a gracious divine endowment), employ it for one another as [befits] good trustees of God's many-sided grace —faithful stewards of the extremely diverse [powers and gifts granted to Christians by] unmerited favor.**

Once you read that verse, there are no more excuses. You have a talent that your pastor and your local church needs to help reach your city. Each church has a vision that was given to the pastor by the Holy Spirit, and the pastor should take the time to share that vision with the church. Then members of the congregation should seek the Lord Jesus Christ to discover where each of them fits into that vision.

Opportunities to get involved are unlimited. Most local churches have departments, activities, or outreach ministries in which each church member would fit. Listed below are some of the departments available in our local church:

| | |
|---|---|
| Academy | Maintenance |
| School of World Evangelism | Marriage Builders |
| Bookstore | Music Ministry |
| Children's Ministry | Prison Ministry |
| Counseling | Publications |
| Counselors in Service | Security |
| Disciples Training Classes | Singles Life I (20-24) |
| Evangelism Ministry | Singles Life II (25-39) |
| Financial Counseling | Singles Life III (40-60) |
| Door Greeters | Sound Department |
| Helping Hands | Tape Duplication |
| Hospital Visitation | Temporarily Impaired |
| Housekeeping | TV-KVTN (Channel 25) |
| Intercession | Ushers |
| Jail Ministry | Visitation |
| "Kids Like You" | Visitor Center |
| Ladies Bible Study | |

Other churches may offer more or fewer avenues of Christian work, but there are always opportunities available that require people willing to release their talents.

## Armorbearers Are Vital for Churches

Without those who do this, the church cannot function, and the Gospel will not be preached to our cities. Pastors and leaders in the majority of churches have been bearing the brunt of the work of the ministry. That is why you hear of so many ministers "burning out."

Pastors and other spiritual leaders should be *breaking through*, not burning out. Spiritual and natural breakthroughs will happen as the Body of Christ decides to do its full part.

I came to Agape Church in Little Rock two weeks after it was started in May of 1979. As soon as I arrived, I began to get involved. I set out to do whatever I could do to help Pastor Happy Caldwell fulfill his vision for the church.

In 1982, we started a mission school to reach around the world. My call was to direct that school and place missionaries wherever the Lord led. One night in 1983, the Lord quickened my heart to read the story of David and Saul. I turned to 1 Samuel 16:21 and read:

**And David came to Saul, and stood before him: and he loved him greatly; and he became his armourbearer.**

At that time, the Lord said to me, "Son, I have called you to be Pastor Caldwell's armorbearer."

An armorbearer carried his leader's shield into battle, and if necessary, he laid down his life for the one whom he served. The shield for me is the vision God birthed into Pastor Caldwell's life.

The Lord said, "Run with the vision I have given him, and I will see to it that yours will be fulfilled."

I am now in my fifteenth year in this ministry, and I am seeing God faithfully fulfill His call on my life. I am blooming where God has planted me.

God is calling for many Christians to become armorbearers for their leaders and for each other. We should begin to work as a team to advance God's Kingdom in the earth.

While preparing to speak to our office and ministerial staff one day, the Holy Spirit put into my heart to ask them each to give me two keys that had produced longevity in their positions and had helped them bloom where they were planted. We have several full-time staff members who have been with the church for many years. The church staff overall has remained very solidly committed.

From that meeting came forty keys to producing longevity of service in the place where God has placed you. Here are those keys in the order in which they were given.

## Successful Keys to Blooming Where You Are Planted

1. You must have a call from God.

2. First of all, make sure you have a real personal relationship with Christ.

3. Ask God to give you His vision, or goal for your life.

4. Be willing to do whatever is asked.

5. Do not lose sight of the people behind the work.

6. Be thankful for your position and never take it for granted.

7. Be willing to submit to authority.

8. Know that you are in God's will.

9. Know that your rewards are laid up in Heaven.

10. Develop a servant's heart.

11. Walk without offense.

12. Serve as if you were serving Jesus Himself, and do not get your eyes on the man under whom you work. On the other hand, be careful to respect the call that is on his life.

13. Be patient.

14. Have a loyalty that goes beyond personal feelings.

15. Respect everyone.

16. Hear no evil, see no evil, and speak no evil.

17. Judge yourself.

18. Do not ever be too big to do the small things or too small to do the big things.

19. Commit to the ministry the way you ought to be committed to your marriage.

20. Know that you are important and needed.

21. Help other people fulfill their ministries.

22. Do everything you know to do to get where you want to be.

23. Do the very best wherever you are.

24. Stay with something until the job is done.

25. Never quit.

26. Be dependable.

27. Be a good follower as well as a good leader.

28. Maintain your joy in the Lord.

29. Always remain sensitive to the Holy Spirit.

30. Always obey God's specific instructions.

31. Be patient with one another.

32. Always walk in love.

33. Be willing to change direction.

34. Know that God is your Source.

35. Use all the abilities that God has given you.

36. Have a healthy perspective of yourself.

37. Always keep the overall vision of the church before you.

38. Maintain a good attitude.

39. Trust in God's grace and His anointing on your life.

40. Be big enough to be rebuked and corrected.

I have divided these forty keys into four separate categories that will help us get a better understanding of them. We will take a look at the most important keys of each category:

- Longevity

- Commitment

- Attitude

- Teamwork

As I begin to share about these four areas, I will be presenting this from the viewpoint of blooming in the local church. These things are what it will take for you to be faithful and to be where God wants you to be. These are working in my life, and I know they will work in yours.

# 2
# Keys to Longevity

The first key to longevity is *understanding the call of God.*

Matthew 13:37,38 says:

> **He answered and said unto them, He that soweth the good seed is the Son of man;**
>
> **The field is the world; the good seed are the children of the kingdom . . . .**

You can see that in God's hands, we are "seed," and the world is His field. He wants us to put our lives in His hands and let Him plant us into the world. God determined the type of seed you are and where you were to be planted.

Genesis 1:11 says that the "seed is in itself." Now, what does that mean? It means that a seed of corn is always going to produce only corn, a kernel of wheat will produce wheat, a grain of rice will produce rice. You cannot get rice from corn. So it is in the mind of God. He planned our lives before the world was created. Now, He wants to plant each of us so we can begin to bloom and bring forth fruit in season.

If you take a quick look at how a seed produces, it will give you some spiritual insight. A seed first is planted in the ground to go through a process of actually dying. Then, a rootlet will begin to push its way through the earth as the rain and sunshine give life to it.

Does that seed ever think, "Am I going to get through all of this dirt on top of me? It is so hard, and I feel hopeless."

But then, one day, it happens. The seed comes forth, and the bud breaks into the sunlight. Many members of the Body of Christ are like that seed — all they see is dirt piled on top of them. Even staff members of ministries sometimes feel mistreated and left out. Perhaps they feel God has forsaken them because all they can see is dirt.

If they will just stay where God planted them and be faithful during the hard times, they will come forth. A seed is destined to spring forth if it is planted in good soil. If you know you are in the will of God and are where He wants you to be, then you *will* come forth, because it is God's destiny at work in you.

God wants His children to grow up and be like trees planted by rivers of water. (Ps. 1:3.) Have you ever noticed something peculiar about a tree? *It never moves!* We have beautiful pine trees on our church property, but I have never driven into the parking lot and found one of those trees had moved overnight to a different place because it did not like where it was planted.

Yet, in the Body of Christ and even on church staffs, the first time someone is offended, he pulls up his roots and moves somewhere else — then wonders why there is no fruit in his life.

If a tree is continually uprooted and replanted, eventually the roots will die. Many Christians have experienced this. Because of rebellion and sin in their hearts, they constantly jump from one church to another. They refuse to submit to authority, or they feel they have special gifts for the church which the pastor is not willing to recognize.

That kind of attitude keeps a person from fulfilling the divine, Heaven-ordained call God placed on his life. We must judge ourselves and be willing to die to our own purposes and dreams to let God's will be done, no matter the personal cost.

Second Timothy 1:9 says:

**Who hath saved us, and called us with a holy calling, not according to our works, but according to his own purpose and grace, which was given us in Christ Jesus before the world began.**

This, to me, is one of the most important scriptures in the Bible as far as understanding your calling. God has saved us and called us. That means if you are born again, you are called. You cannot stand before Jesus one day and say, "I was never called." He saved you and called you, according to His own purpose and grace.

## God Has a Purpose for You

God has a purpose in life for you to fulfill. You are not here by accident. You have a destiny in God to fulfill. You must find out your purpose by seeking God. Then, you become the deciding factor in fulfilling that purpose.

It was the God-ordained, God-destined time for the children of Israel to go into the promised land when God took them there from Egypt. However, because of doubt and unbelief, they missed their purpose in life.

For forty years, the Israelites walked in circles in the wilderness until all of the males older than twenty years had died. People with no purposes tend to walk in circles, blaming their failures on God or someone else. They walk until they dig holes for themselves and eventually die. Then, many times, they die full of bitterness, mad at other people and God.

Joshua and Caleb, the only two men of that generation to live to see the promised land, were of a different spirit. They knew they had a purpose and a call on their lives and that, by faith in God, they could possess the land.

I really feel sorry for Joshua and Caleb because they had to wait forty years to take what rightfully belonged to them.

They could have been enjoying their destiny, but they had to wait because of the rebellion of others.

Second Timothy 1:9 says God's purpose and grace was given to us in Christ before the world ever began. God knew who you were before you were born. Before He ever said, "Light be," He knew you in His omnipotent mind. He had a reason for your being born in the generation in which you were born.

I got real honest with God one day, and I asked Him while in prayer, "I want to know why I am here? I want to know why I was born into the Nance family? Why am I here at this time?"

You see, you had nothing to do with it. God did not ask your opinion when He planned you and made you. It was all up to Him. Why were we not born in the days of Abraham, Moses, David, or even Jesus? Why were we not born in the fifteenth, sixteenth, or seventeenth centuries? Why did God put us in this last generation?

I believe, when God created the world, He saw a time period in which sin would abound as never before, a time when great calamities would happen on the earth. He foresaw a time when the greatest deception would come to try the people of God, and a time when gross darkness would come on many people, and the love of many would wax cold.

In the midst of seeing all this, I believe God said to Himself, "I am going to raise up a people who will not compromise My Word, a people with My Spirit, anointing, and joy to go forth in those days and usher in the greatest move of My Spirit the world has ever seen. I will pour out My Spirit upon all flesh and raise up a glorious Church without spot or wrinkle." (Eph. 5:27.)

When God determined these things, He said it would be a "special" people to live in these days, and in His mind,

He saw *you*. He saw you and put you in place for a divine purpose.

No matter what position you hold, you are there to produce for the Kingdom of God and bring the lost into the saving knowledge of Jesus. We must realize that we were called before we met our families, our spouses, or anyone else in our lives. And we must, at the Judgment, give account to God for what we did with that purpose and calling.

> **For we must all appear before the judgment seat of Christ; that everyone may receive the things done in his body, according to that he hath done, whether it be good or bad.**
>
> **2 Corinthians 5:10**

It is an awesome thing to think that I will stand before Jesus and give an account of what I did with the gifts and calling on my life. My pastor will not be able to stand up for me and say that I was a good associate. My wife will not be able to testify that I was a good husband. Only I can answer the Lord.

He will say, "Terry, what did you do with what I gave you. Did you fulfill your assignment?"

My assignment at this point is to be the senior associate and missions director of Agape Church, Inc. The Lord has told me to take the same vision, anointing, and integrity of this church and reproduce it in the world.

## All Will Give An Account

To you who are reading this book, I say by the Spirit of God, "As surely as you are reading this, you too will stand before Him and answer the same questions."

That is why our callings are so important and why we must endure hardships if they come while fulfilling them. We must be determined to have God's will in our lives no matter the cost. Hebrews 5:7 says:

> **Who in the days of his flesh, when he had offered
> up prayers and supplications with strong crying and
> tears unto him that was able to save him from death,
> and was heard in that he feared.**

Jesus went through strong crying and tears to fulfill
God's will. Many church and ministry staff personnel run
from anything that is hard and say, if it is the will of God, it
would be easy! Well, welcome to the real world. It takes
strong crying and tears sometimes to stay where God
plants you and refuse to move no matter the conditions.

In building longevity in your life, another priority is
your *personal relationship with Christ*. It is easy to stay so
involved with the work of the ministry that our lives seem
to be racing ahead of us. It is easy to be so caught up with
the work of the ministry that we overlook our intimate
times with Jesus.

I find it very interesting that in Luke 11:1, the disciples
asked Jesus to teach them how to pray. Jesus' ministry was
very well-known at that time, with miracles, signs, and
wonders occurring all of the time. However, the Bible never
says that the disciples even one time asked Jesus for His
*anointing*.

Today, we see great men of God flowing in major
healing and deliverance anointings. It is amazing how
many people I hear who desire, covet, want — and would
do anything — if these ministers would lay hands on them
and "transfer" the anointing.

No one alive has ever flowed in the gifts of the Holy
Spirit to the degree that Jesus did. If we covet that kind of
anointing, we must do as the disciples did and ask Jesus
how to pray. We must follow the pattern set by Jesus.
Ministers are falling because they lost their intimacy with
the Lord. Many have fallen into sin simply because they
substituted work of the ministry for an intimate
relationship.

When in prayer one day, the Lord revealed to me the key to seeing the calling on my life fulfilled. It is by intimacy, pregnancy, travail, and birth. Spiritual life is born into the earth following the same pattern as natural life is born. We must become "intimate" with God. From that intimacy comes "pregnancy."

That means we are pregnant with the visions and plans God has for our lives. Then, we must travail. *To travail* means "to intercede, care for, pray, and speak God's Word over that vision or plan. The travailing comes first; then, the children are born.

We get God's plan, will, and direction by establishing a habit of prayer and study of the Word. Pressures are coming at Christians today in a greater intensity than we have ever experienced. That is because the devil knows his time is short. The key to our being able to walk in victory is to cry out, "Lord, teach us to pray."

## Those Who Seek God Will Follow a Vision

You will have many opportunities to quit the position you hold. I have had times of trial and hardship when I prayed for God to let me leave! And I found that the strength to stand, strength to go on, and strength to resist Satan only comes in prayer. In our quiet times with God, He gives peace and strength.

We must develop a heart that seeks after God. David, King of Israel, was known as a man whose heart followed after God. If we could interview him today, we might ask what his greatest goal was in life:

- Was it to be the greatest king?
- Was it to be the greatest musician?
- Was it to be the wealthiest man on earth?

David's answer would be one of his psalms:

> One thing have I desired of the Lord, that will I
> seek after; that I may dwell in the house of the Lord all
> the days of my life, to behold the beauty of the Lord,
> and to inquire in his temple.
>
> Psalm 27:4

David's quest in life was to have God's heart. If we are ever to be true successes in God's Kingdom, we also must know that our first ministry is to glorify and honor Him. First Peter 2:5 says that we are a holy priesthood, and we are to offer up spiritual sacrifices, acceptable to God by Christ Jesus.

The first calling for all of us is to worship and honor the Lord on a daily basis. Jesus prayed to the Father. He had a habit of prayer. That was the key to His anointing, wisdom, and longevity.

> And he came out, and went, as he was wont (as was
> his habit) to the mount of Olives (to pray); and his
> disciples followed him.
>
> Luke 22:39

Another important part of longevity is *having a vision and a goal*. I heard a man say, "I would rather have high goals and reach half of them than to have no goals and reach all of them."

Second Kings 4:1-3 says:

> Now there cried a certain woman of the wives of
> the sons of the prophets unto Elisha, saying, Thy
> servant my husband is dead; and thou knowest that thy
> servant did fear the Lord: and the creditor is come to
> take unto him my two sons to be bondmen.
>
> And Elisha said unto her, What shall I do for thee?
> tell me, what hast thou in the house? And she said,
> Thine handmaid hath not anything in the house, save a
> pot of oil.
>
> Then he said, Go, borrow thee vessels abroad of all
> thy neighbors, even empty vessels; borrow not a few.

That widow was left with a choice: She could go and get a lot of vessels, or she could borrow just a few. She gathered vessels and began to pour the oil. When did the oil stop? It stopped when she ran out of jars. She held the key to her miracle.

She could have said, "It is too hot today to gather jars," or, "Elisha, I don't feel well," or "I could only find one jar."

Whatever she brought in is what she received. If she had really known what God was about to do, she could have found a dry well and said, "That is my jar!"

Elisha would have laughed, and I believe God would have laughed as well. If you do not exercise faith in life to reach a goal or vision, you will never achieve it. You are going to have to get up and work toward your goal. God blesses what you do.

When I first came on staff at Agape, I did not know exactly what my goal and vision was for God. I knew that I had a desire for the mission field but that was all. As I was becoming part of a new church, I could not expect to be sent immediately to the mission field. So I began by just locking and unlocking the church building and getting things ready before every service.

That was a small goal but still a responsibility God gave me to do, and I did that for three years until He raised up a full-time person to take care of it. In the meantime, doors to the mission field began to open. *You must start with what your hand finds to do.* (Eccl. 9:10.)

If you will go to your pastor or church leaders and begin to serve them, the vision God has for you will begin to come to pass. Be a blessing in your local church, and you will find doors opening up in all directions.

Everyone in some way must be connected with a local body under the leadership of a God-called pastor in the days to come. Many people move from one ministry to the next, based on what they think each has to offer them — never asking what God wants.

## Stay Where God Puts You

*Knowing that you are in the ministry that God intends* for you is yet another key to longevity. I believe this is the decade of the local church. Using ministries as stepping stones is wrong, and that could be the reason you are not prospering in your call. This key applies to everyone, not just full-time ministers.

When I graduated from Southwestern Assembly of God Bible College, I received a very good offer. The dean of the college told me that he wanted to recommend me to a very good church that would have been a great opportunity. However, I had real peace in my heart about attending Rhema Bible Training Center in Broken Arrow, Oklahoma, near Tulsa.

I knew that, if we moved to Tulsa, it would mean both my wife and I would have to find jobs. This move would be a real test of faith for us, especially when I had the opportunity to move immediately into full-time ministry.

Friends would say, "Why are you going to a Bible school? You just graduated from college!"

But God had another plan. He was preparing my way to Little Rock via Tulsa. We must follow our hearts and not the offers. God holds the future, and the best future for you does not always hold what seems to be the best offer. The will of God is to stay planted where God has you until He says to move.

This leads to another key to longevity, which is *making God your complete Source.* Every Christian will be faced with a situation in which to make a decision to either trust God or to trust man. Jeremiah 17:5-8 says:

Thus saith the Lord; Cursed be the man that trusteth in man, and maketh flesh his arm, and whose heart departeth from the Lord.

For he shall be like the heath in the desert, and shall not see when good cometh; but shall inhabit the parched places in the wilderness, in a salt land and not inhabited.

Blessed is the man that trusteth in the Lord, and whose hope the Lord is.

For he shall be as a tree planted by the waters, and that spreadeth out her roots by the river, and shall not see when heat cometh, but her leaf shall be green; and shall not be careful in the year of drought, neither shall cease from yielding fruit.

We did move to Tulsa and rented a small apartment. My wife, Kim, got a job, and I worked part-time as youth director in a church. But we were barely making it. At one time, for two weeks, all we had in the house was about eight dozen eggs given us by Kim's aunt. The bills were paid, but we had no money for food.

When I realized that we had to eat eggs for two weeks, I wanted to cry for help from my mom and dad. I knew all I had to do was pick up the phone and the money would be on its way. However, I also knew that would be trusting in my parents and not in God.

After a few days, I thought that I would sprout feathers: We had fried eggs, scrambled eggs, boiled eggs, and poached eggs. Then I got a call from the pastor of a church with about a thousand members asking me to come work for him. The salary looked like a heaven-sent one, and I thought perhaps God wanted me to leave Tulsa and take that job.

I told the pastor I would come and visit with him about the job, but when I hung up the phone, Kim began to cry.

She said, "Terry, you know God wants us here. We can't even go down there and talk to the pastor about this."

After we prayed, I had to call the pastor back and apologize for even offering to come visit him about that job. I told him I knew God had called me to be in Tulsa. Then I hung up, looked at Kim, and said, "Pass the eggs."

I do not regret that decision, because that is how God taught me to trust Him. Even when I arrived in Little Rock and talked with the Caldwells, we knew it was a step of faith. They knew we were supposed to join them, and Kim and I knew God was telling us to come. We came with no mention of salary, just knowing by the inner peace that God would supply, and He has.

You must have a revelation in your heart that your church is not your source, your pastor is not your source, and your salary is not your source. Every Christian will face times when it is necessary to find out who to trust: God or man. If you lean toward man, then man will be the limit of your supply.

I have known people who volunteered to help in a local church, working for no pay but doing it unto the Lord. Then, because of their faithfulness, they were placed on staff. Now they were getting paid but were expected to be on time and put in a full day's work. Their attitudes began to be that the church owed them something. They felt they were worth more than they were paid, and the work demands were too much. They lost sight of Who they were working for and Who was their real Source.

Do not allow anger to rise up in you against your pastor or your employer when you find yourself in a situation where you must believe God financially. If you agreed to work for the salary offered by the ministry, you have no right to get angry when you face a situation of lack.

Your source of supply must be God.

# Trust and Obey

Two other keys for longevity are *trusting in God's grace on your life* and *always obey God's original instructions.*

You have a grace on your life and talents and abilities to do what God has called you to do. You may not understand or realize your talents at first, but eventually, if you persist, you will see them.

First Corinthians 15:10 says:

> **But by the grace of God I am what I am: and his grace which was bestowed upon me was not in vain; but I laboured more abundantly than they all: yet not I, but the grace of God which was with me.**

When I first came to work at Agape Church and sat down with Pastor Caldwell, he asked me what my talents were. I was embarrassed and really had nothing to say. As far as I knew, I had little talent.

So I looked at him and said, "The only thing I can tell you is that I will be faithful, dependable, and never be late."

He said, "That is what I am looking for."

At that point, I began to see the grace of God, and understanding His grace is a humbling experience. When he takes your life, anoints you, and makes you into something you never thought you could be, that is His grace in operation.

When I wrote *God's Armorbearer* [Tulsa: Harrison House, Inc., 1990], I was concerned that no one would ever read it. I wondered why God had asked me to write it, because I do not claim to be a writer.

When the first seven thousand and five hundred copies arrived, we stacked the boxes in a storage room. I closed the door, got down on my knees, and almost begged God to sell those books. It has been a real blessing to me to see God use that book in the way that he has. Currently, it has remained a bestseller being sold worldwide in four languages.

You also have talents in your life that will come forth as you trust God's grace in the small things. We are what we are by His grace. If you always *obey* His original instructions, you will see things begin to work.

Many times, because of an over-zealousness to do great things for God, we start getting off the course He has set for us. We want to dream big dreams, and then go after those dreams. The problem with that is when you wake up one day and find out it was not God's dream but your own.

Following your own dream will lead to a dead-end street, usually with a lot of time and money wasted. You must stop and take a look at what God originally told you to do in the beginning. Go back to what He spoke to your heart. There is where you will find the peace of God and His prosperity.

Today it is easy for a Christian to say, "I feel led to do this," and "I feel led to do that." People move from one thing to another always "feeling led," but never Holy-Spirit-led.

A pastor told me once that he was so tired of having people come in his office saying "I feel led" that he was going to get a large chunk of lead to put on his desk. The next time someone said that, he was going to rub the lead and say, "So do I!"

If the Lord has told you to join a church and commit yourself there, then do exactly what He said. Determine to be the greatest blessing to your church that anyone ever has been. From there, God will direct you one step at a time, and you will not miss Him. We will not miss God, if we will learn to walk in the Spirit and stay with what God originally told us to do.

# Patience and Flexibility

*Patience* is another key to longevity. Patience means "the suffering of afflictions, pain, toil, calamity, provocation or other evil with a calm, unfurled temper." Patience also means enduring without murmuring or fretting. Or it is the act, or quality, of waiting long for justice or expected good without discontent. Romans 12:6,7 says:

> **Having then gifts differing according to the grace that is given to us whether prophecy, let us prophesy according to the proportion of faith;**
>
> **Or ministry,** *let us wait on our ministering. . . .*

You can see where a lot of problems come from in our lives: We are not patient. We are not willing to endure hardships, and we always are looking for an opportunity to be personally exalted and promoted. The Bible says to *wait on our ministering.* God wants to develop His character in you first before He exalts your ministry. However, we usually like promotion first and character later.

As you determine to have the will of God operate in your life, and you get connected to a local church, the opportunities to murmur, complain, and become impatient will be there. Most of these feelings usually are directed to those in authority over us. We feel that *we* have a call and a place, and our pastors are not letting our gifts come forth.

That does happen occasionally, if you run into a pastor who is a controlling-type person. But, the bottom line even then is: Did God call you there? If He did, it probably was for the purpose of learning patience.

I have found that when I really want something to happen for me, when I really want a new door to open up, I first have to give it to the Lord. It is amazing that, when you do that, it will not be long until the door opens. You must relax in God and in ministry and let His perfect timing take place. It is by faith and patience that you will receive the promise.

Along with patience, you must have flexibility. That means *being willing to change.* We must be careful not to get in a rut. A rut is simply an elongated grave.

The majority of people in the world prefer to be "secure," which means keeping their own little "worlds" stable with little change. Because of this characteristic of human nature, we easily can get "tunnel vision" and miss the prompting of the Holy Spirit to make a change in our churches or in our lives.

If you look at what happened in the Church from the sixties right up to the present, you can see God moving in a different way in each decade.

In the sixties, God began to pour out His Spirit on all denominations and the Charismatic Movement resulted. The seventies brought a revival of the office of the teacher. Teaching centers began to spring up around the country. Then the eighties brought a new commitment and a call to emphasize local churches. Thus far in the nineties, the Lord has turned our attention to the harvest of the lost.

We can see from this how the Holy Spirit changes direction, and you can see why we need to follow His leading to get located for this last-day harvest. If you are going to be in the move of God, you must find out where He is moving and follow Him.

In your church, you will face many opportunities to change, and the changes may come in a way that will require time for you to adjust. In order for us and our churches to grow, we must be open to search our own hearts and let changes perfect us.

I believe God is challenging us to take steps of faith that we have never taken before. God wants to move us out of our comfort zones. The purpose is to open your ministry to reach more people. The children of Israel had it made as long as God put a cloud over them during the day to protect them from the desert sun, a fire at night to warm them, and manna to feed them.

At least, they had it made until God said it was time to change. He told them to possess the promised land. But He was going to take away their "securities," and they were going to have to fight and take the land by faith. What happened? They rebelled in unbelief. Why? It was time to make changes, and they were comfortable just the way they were.

Your life and ministry will stop dead in its tracks if you do not accept change. You will never accomplish what God has for you if you get comfortable. If you are going to reach out and minister to this generation, you will never do it with a sixties, seventies, or eighties mentality. You may be more comfortable with the way things were, but this generation thinks differently.

The Church must get with God and find out His strategies for reaching this generation. The ministries that do this are the ones that will move into the harvest years ahead of us.

# 3
# Keys to Commitment

The first key to commitment is *a loyalty and faithfulness* that goes beyond *all* personal feelings. The dictionary defines *loyalty* as being "faithful to a prince or a superior, true to a plighted (vowed or sworn to) faith, duty, or love." Faithfulness is defined as "firmly adhering to duty, loyal, true to one's allegiance," or as being "a faithful subject."

These definitions show the heart of an armorbearer. This is someone willing to give of himself for others. He is dependable and loyal to his leaders and can be trusted with difficult assignments. Loyalty and faithfulness, of course, are first to God and then to man.

The Prophet Daniel and the three Hebrew children refused to eat the rich food usually served to the king's table when they were taken captive to Babylon. A lot of the food was totally against the dietary laws given to Moses by God. I have wondered why the other young captives did not follow their example.

When you think about it, however, you can hardly blame them. Their country had been destroyed, their family members probably all killed or least also held captive, and they were prisoners in a strange city. Perhaps they thought God had forsaken them and there no longer was reason to hold onto His laws. But Daniel remained faithful, and as a result, he was highly exalted in the middle of an ungodly nation.

Today, as a staff member of a church or ministry, when you are asked by a pastor or church leader to do something or change something, you are not a prisoner in an alien land as was Daniel. Your attitude to those over you is a test of your loyalty to God.

Loyalty always is tested first where God is concerned. If you do not like something a superior asks you to do, you may think it is between you and him. But it is really between you and God, if you are where God has put you. Make changes in your attitude and in your obedience to God, and then doing what you are asked to do will not bother you.

Personal feelings must be laid aside when you make a decision to serve God in whatever ministry He puts you. After all, He knew all of the rules and regulations of that ministry before He put you there.

Faithfulness is something that has to be found, according to 1 Corinthians 4:2. The Bible says to know those who labor among you. That is why your pastor and church leaders watch for faithfulness. When they find someone who has proven himself trustworthy in hard and difficult situations, they know that person is mature and can handle more responsibility.

Take a look at four characteristics of a faithful man:

1. A faithful man knows how to keep his mouth shut. (Prov. 11:13.)

2. A faithful man ministers strength to his pastor and church. (Prov. 13:17.)

3. A faithful man always will speak the truth. (Prov. 14:5.)

4. A faithful man is a humble man. (Prov. 20:6.)

No one works in or is a member of a perfect church. Nor are pastors perfect. It is hard to be faithful at times while working with imperfect people. On the other hand, if you examine your own life, you may find you are not as perfected as you think. But Jesus died on the cross for imperfect people, so we could all have divine life with Him. We are to give ourselves in the same way to bring people into the perfect Kingdom, which is God's.

## Do Not Be Too Big or Too Small

Another key to commitment is: *Don't ever be too big to do the small, but don't ever be too small to do the big.* While teaching this to our staff that day, this point came from our Children's Minister. When he came on staff, he was called to work with children. He was very content and happy with what he was doing. But one day, he was asked to be on our children's TV program called, "Kids Like You."

Now this was all new to him. He thought, "There is no way I could ever be on TV and play a role as one of the main characters."

But God was stretching him to expand him into a new area for the purpose of reaching more children. It is always in God's plan to exalt you, but you will find you will have to expand. He had never once thought or desired to do that, but God had a plan. Sometimes we can miss God because we see more responsibility, and we are afraid we cannot handle it.

Now, on the other hand, we cannot get to the place that we are too big to do the small. There is an attitude in some leaders because of who they are that excuses them to do whatever they want and say whatever they want. But the Bible is very clear that they have a judge also.

There is a law that works for masters and servants alike — you reap what you sow. (Gal. 6:7.) Get lifted up by pride, and you are destined to fall. (Prov. 16:18.) If you are unteachable, you open the door to deception. Paul wrote that we should not think of ourselves more highly than we ought. (Rom. 12:3.) Once we begin to think we are better than others, problems begin. Determine to keep a humble heart and think soberly about yourself, and God will exalt you.

Another key to commitment is *committing to the ministry as you are committed to your marriage*. Of course, your marriage comes before your position in the church; however, you should approach the work for the Lord with the same fervency.

Concerning commitment, I heard a story of a farmer with a chicken and a pig who loved him because he was so good to them.

On the farmer's birthday, the chicken went to the pig and said, "Let's do something special for him," and the pig said, "That sounds great, but what can we do?"

The chicken said, "Let's serve him breakfast. I'll give him eggs, and you can give him bacon."

The pig said, "Wait a minute. You are only giving an offering, but you're asking *total commitment* out of me!"

It will require a total commitment to be faithful and do what you are called to do. The strongest key to having a successful marriage is communication. Likewise, in working with your pastor and leaders, communication is a must. The reason for misunderstandings is a lack of communication. Jesus always took the time to communicate with His disciples. He knew the continuation of His ministry depended on it.

This need for communication works both ways, of course. Workers need to let pastors and leaders know of potential problems, and pastors must take the time to put their hearts into their people. If a pastor is truly joined to his flock as a shepherd, the sheep will know his voice. A congregation of people cry for security. That comes from a commitment to a pastor, and that pastor making a commitment back to the people.

# Always Do Your Best

*Doing your best* is another key to commitment. A pastor is always concerned about whether his staff and his congregation feel about the church the way he does. The way you can minister peace to him, as an armorbearer, is to always do your best.

A visitor walked into our church one morning with a crying child in her arms. The woman seemed upset, so one of our nursery workers took the child and told her to go on into the service. The woman made Jesus Lord of her life at the end of the service. That nursery worker saw a situation and did her best to help. When she stands before Jesus, she has a great reward waiting.

Colossians 3:23,24 says to do whatever you do heartily as unto the Lord and not unto men in order to receive the reward of the inheritance.

The final two keys to commitment:

1. *Stay with something until the job gets done.*

2. *Never quit or give up.*

If you are working in any department in a church, and you are given a job to do — just do it! Then, make sure it is completely finished. Many times we want to start a new project before the last one is finished.

You will have many opportunities to quit. They present themselves often. It takes no effort to quit; that is the easy way out. When God told me to be my pastor's armorbearer, no exceptions were included.

When we began to build the present church building, the Lord said to construct it "debt-free." Making a decision like that means a lot of work depends on the voluntary efforts of staff and congregation. It meant work days every Saturday. And, when we moved from the shopping center store-front church to the new building, it had no ceiling, no carpet, and an echo problem that was unbelievable.

Chairs had to be set up before every service and taken down afterwards, along with all of the sound and band equipment. Construction crews would come in the day after a service and make a huge mess. The floors would be covered in dust, so they had to be swept before every service. At times, we may have looked as if we were covered with a "glory cloud," but it was really sheet-rock dust.

When we began, we had plenty of volunteers, but as the weeks and months passed, it seemed only a few were left to help. It was my responsibility to make sure it was done. During this time, there were not many days to just relax. But I look back at it and would not trade that time for anything — although I am glad it is over. The "hardship" pulled things out of me that I did not know were there. Some were good, and some not so good. But through it, I learned the only way to succeed is never to quit.

When the carpet was finally laid, I got down on my knees and kissed it! That was the most beautiful sight I think I have ever seen.

If you are truly committed to the church and pastor where God has sent you, then you will not quit when you face hard times. The reality is that you will face challenges in the growth of your church that will test your commitment, whether you are a member or a pastor.

You will have the privilege of dealing with pride, anger, bitterness, selfishness, and all the destructive things that are in human behavior. But, once you learn to deal with these, overcome them, and let God begin a work in you, then you will become more like Him.

God is preparing you for leadership. The key is to stay committed to God, your call, and the leaders set over you.

# 4
# Keys to Attitude

The first key to attitude is *a willingness to do whatever you are asked*. This is what leaders look for in people who desire to get involved. This is an attitude we all must develop in our hearts when we work in the Kingdom of God. You may not think you have the talent or ability to do whatever is asked, but you will set yourself to do it *because* you were asked.

Not long after coming to this church, I was asked to take care of the weekly bulletin. I have no artistic ability. The last time I did anything with art was pasting valentines in the fifth grade! But I told Pastor Caldwell I would be happy to do it. It took me a while, but I did it to the best of my ability because the church needed it done. Later, someone else came along with the necessary talent and took over that job.

Another time, I asked someone to help me with something, but that person said, "I'm sorry, but that is not my 'grace' gift."

That may have been so, but I was asking for help — not a word from God. However, that is the kind of attitude many people have in local churches, and that is why they are never used. What is on the inside of a person is more important than what is on the outside. The greatest blessing to me is when people come and say they are joining our church and want to know where they can help. Those are the people who end up in leadership positions.

The next key to the right attitude is *never lose sight of the people behind the work.* This thought came from one of our computer operators, who sits day after day keying information for the ministry into our computers. She said the Lord has helped her not to just type in name after name, but to be concerned about these people and to pray for them. You must not let what you do in the church turn into just another job.

Church workers must get a revelation of the people involved. They must know that they are working for *people*, loving *people*, and daily giving their lives for *people*, all of whom God loves. Without people, there would be no churches. People are the reason we are called to work in the Kingdom.

For example, it takes a lot of work to get ready for our annual Campmeeting. Sometimes, the best feeling about Campmeeting is when it is over! But, that was a wrong attitude, and it came because I let myself get caught up in all of the work and responsibility. My focus was not on people.

I am sure there were times when the disciples felt the same way, perhaps after Jesus fed thousands of men with loaves and fishes, not counting the women and children. When those meals were over and the leftovers gathered up in baskets, I expect that the disciples were glad. But, just think, they had a part in a wonderful miracle.

That is what you must always think: "Here is an opportunity to minister to more people, and God is letting me have a part."

If you get upset at all of the work you have to do, then you need to judge your heart's attitude. You are losing sight of the *people*. All of that work is changing people's eternal destiny, so it is worth it.

## Be Thankful in All Things

A third key to having the right attitude is *being thankful for your position and retaining your joy*. We should always be thankful for the place in which God has put us. The Apostle Paul wrote that we should give thanks in everything, because it is the will of God for us. (1 Thess. 5:18.) You may want a change in your life and position, but that will only come when you learn to be thankful for where you are. We are not just to be thankful in good times, but even during difficult times.

I learned a valuable lesson on being thankful when I visited a missionary couple from our church living in northern Romania. The lifestyle there is like going back in time a hundred years in this country. This couple must do all of their cooking and baking by hand, and they have five children.

While there, they are responsible for raising up a church and a Bible School. For the first four months, they had no hot water, and when they finally got a hot water tank, it broke after working a while. Then it took several weeks to get it fixed.

Watching things that went on, I asked, "How do you make it?" They looked at me and spoke a revelation to my heart when they said, "We have learned to be thankful. If we have no *hot* water, then we thank God for any water at all. We pray in the Spirit one hour a day, and then we thank God continually."

That is an attitude that will cause you to win in any situation. The victory begins in thanksgiving.

Paul wrote in Phillippians 1:15-19 of some people who were preaching from the wrong heart with the purpose of adding afflictions to Paul, who was in prison at the time. But he did not develop the wrong attitude in return. Instead, he rejoiced over the fact that Christ was at least being preached.

If you have problems now in your ministry or work, begin to rejoice. That will bring you strength, and your strength will minister to everyone around you. You will have to fight to keep it, but it is yours. Joy is not determined by circumstances.

Paul learned that lesson years before when he and Silas were beaten with "many stripes" and cast into prison with their feet fastened in the stocks. But they prayed and sang praises to God, even at midnight, and there was a great earthquake which shook the foundations of the prison. The doors were opened, and everyone's bands were loosed. (Acts 16:23-26.)

Take a close look at the faith they exercised. Their backs were bleeding, they had been put in stocks, and all this for doing God's will. What a golden opportunity to complain and murmur. In the natural, if they were going to complain, this was the time to start. But, instead, they began to worship God.

I personally believe that Paul might have looked at Silas and asked how he was doing. In response, Silas said, "I'm in pain, but I'm going to make it."

Then Paul said, "Silas, let's do something that is probably the most ridiculous thing you have ever heard of at a time like this. Let's start praising God."

I am sure Silas said, "Paul, you're right. That is the most ridiculous thing I have ever heard. But, let's do it in faith, I'm with you."

I can imagine Jesus looking at the Father and saying, "Do You hear Our servants Paul and Silas giving Us praise? I know they are in pain, and I know they are suffering for My cause, but listen to their faith."

And God was so moved that He sent an earthquake, and *everyone's* bands were loosed. If you need doors to open, then begin to worship God and thank Him for Who He is. From that kind of praise will come deliverance for you, which will effect those around you. Hebrews 13:15

says we are to offer the sacrifice of praise continually, which is the fruit of our lips giving thanks.

## A Servant's Heart Makes a Good Attitude

The next key to having a good attitude is *having a servant's heart*. Jesus told the disciples that, in the Kingdom of God, those who are "chief" are those who serve. He told them that He was among them as One who served. (Luke 22:25-27.) Jesus had a true servant's heart. Christians will never graduate from being servants.

Look at the life of Elisha, who began his ministry by acting as a servant for Elijah for a number of years. When Jehosophat, king of Judah, asked if there was not a prophet in the nation of Israel to go to for advice from the Lord, Elisha was named. However, it was not the miracles he had done or his powerful anointing that was mentioned. (2 Kings 3:10-12.)

A servant of the King of Israel said, "Here is Elisha, the son of Shaphat, *who poured water on the hands of Elijah.*"

In other words, it was his role as servant to a great man that was his recommendation. Elisha was Elijah's armorbearer.

That phrase "who poured water over Elijah's hands" became real to me when I visited Mike Croslow, one of our missionaries in Uganda. He took me out in the bush to preach in a village where there was no running water or electricity. It was not the end of the world, but you felt it was visible from that place!

We preached under a mango tree to hundreds of people and had a wonderful time. When it was time for lunch, we went into a small mud church and sat down at a table. I did not see any utensils, so I asked Mike if there were any.

He said, "No, brother, you get the honor of eating with your hands."

Then a young boy of about fourteen carried in a pitcher of water and a bar of soap. As the guest, he came to me first, handed me the soap and began to pour water over my hands. Then he continued around the room to all of the other ministers who were there. After that, food was brought in, and we prayed and ate. When we finished, the young man came back and poured water again to wash our hands.

After that experience, I understood better the culture of the Middle East in the days of Elijah and Elisha. The younger man would prepare the prophet's meal, bring water and pour it over Elijah's hands before he ate and after. He kept his house, did the cooking, and all of the other menial tasks required. Elisha truly had a servant's heart.

As you learn to serve, the anointing of God will increase on your life to help others. David became king and had a great anointing, but he first experienced God while tending sheep. He was willing to give his life to protect his father's sheep.

He watched that flock with a servant's heart and a watchful eye. You do not hear him complaining about having to take care of some stinking sheep. Because he passed the test of serving with the sheep, he was able to pass the test of Goliath when it came.

Now, what is *your* flock? Is it watching a group of toddlers every Sunday morning? Is it directing a choir, youth group, or children's church? Are you involved in housecleaning, door greeting, or ushering?

Your flock, or area of responsibility, is your "proving ground." If you function well as a servant, you will be promoted.

That brings us to a related key, which is to *serve as if you were serving Jesus*. From the Word of God, you can see clearly that the Bible says we are to work as if we are working for Jesus. If you will get your eyes off your boss and strive to please God first, then you will please your boss. We must learn to see Jesus as our Eternal Employer.

## Understanding Authority

**Servants, obey in all things your masters according to the flesh; not with eyeservice, as menpleasers; but in singleness of heart, fearing God:**

**And whatsoever ye do, do it heartily, as to the Lord, and not unto men.**

**Colossians 3:22,23**

If Jesus asked you to clean the church bathrooms, how clean would they be?

If Jesus asked you to drive a bus on the church bus route, would you be on time?

If Jesus asked you to help in the church nursery, how well would you handle and treat the children?

If Jesus asked you to pray for your church and leadership, how fervently would you pray?

If Jesus asked you to get involved in your local church, how quickly would you respond?

When you volunteer and are asked to do something, you need to remember that it is as if Jesus Himself asked you, because you are doing whatever you do for Him.

This leads us to the attitude of *submitting to God's delegated authority in our lives*. Romans 13:1,2 says that authority is ordained of God and whoever resists authority is resisting God.

God established all authority in chains of command under Him. On this earth, from world governments to church governments, obedience to higher authority is ordained by God. Heaven is run under a principle of authority: God the Father, God the Son, and God the Holy Spirit, then the archangels, cherubs and seraphims, who are submitted to authority over them.

Now, if Michael the archangel tells an angel to go take care of a situation on earth, that angel does not say, "But I only take orders from Gabriel." He would never do that, because he remembers very clearly what happened to the last groups of angels who acted that way.

All *offices* of authority are set up by God, and the authority rests on the office, not the man. We are to submit ourselves to the office, whether or not we like the man in the office. If he misuses his office, we can pray for him to change or pray him out.

In order to properly submit to authority, you must have a clear understanding that the authority rests in the office, not the man. If a president is voted out of office in this country, he no longer has authority in what goes on. A former president cannot just drive up to the White House and walk into the Oval Office without going through the proper security protocol than can the most ordinary citizen. Why? That is because he no longer is in authority.

When God told Moses to speak to the rock in Numbers 20:8-29, we see Moses and Aaron both in rebellion against what God had commanded. Moses angrily struck the rock instead of speaking to it, and Aaron stood with him in this rebellion. Well, God told Moses to bring Aaron and his son, Eleazar, to Mount Hor. There, Moses was instructed by God to take the high priest's robe off of Aaron and place it on Eleazar. When that happened, Aaron died. This shows us what happens when we misrepresent God before people. The authority on the high priest's office remained, but it was now on Eleazar.

When we submit to people and to authority, we submit to the office. The only right we have not to submit to authority is when that authority directly violates the Word of God. When we are asked to do something that is in direct violation of the Word of God, then we do not submit, because we have a *higher* authority.

But, let's be real honest, that is not usually the case. Rebellion usually starts when you have to submit to the rules in your church nursery. That is where it begins. Then it goes into the requirements of joining the church, and when you finally get through that, you are faced with what it takes to be an usher, door greeter, housekeeper, sing in the choir, play in the band, teach in Sunday school, and so on.

Another type of authority which plays a major part in many local churches is: *That is the way we do it around here.* Wherever you go, you will be faced with this "authority." And it does not matter whether you agree with the way things are done or not, you must submit if you know God wants you to be a part of that church or ministry.

If you get mad and begin to speak against the pastor and leaders, then you are in rebellion. You are not coming against the people in those offices; you are coming against God. If you have a problem with something, take the time and make the effort to go talk with the leadership in an attitude of love and let them explain why they operate the way they do.

## Five Structures of Authority

There are five structures of authority that we all must submit to:

1. *God and His Word* (1 John 2:3,4)

We must keep God's Word in our hearts and fully submit to the laws laid down in the Word of God. The reason is that we will be judged according to the Bible, so our lives must line up with the Bible as God's Word.

2. *National and local government* (1 Pet. 2:13,14)

The Apostle Peter wrote that Christians must submit to *every* ordinance of man for the Lord's sake. For example, if you work, you must pay taxes and file with the Internal Revenue Service. Otherwise, you may go to jail. You may not like this, but you have to do it, because it is the law. If we rebel against paying those taxes, we really are rebelling against God and not man. On the other hand, if laws are passed forbidding us to preach, then the national laws have rebelled against God, and we have a higher authority to obey.

### 3. *The church*

One day in 1980, I was sitting in my office at the church reading my Bible, when I heard the Spirit of God say, "Have a Pastor's Appreciation Day."

I had never heard of such a thing. I was raised in church, but we never did anything like that. So I told the rest of the staff, and we worked it all out.

One Sunday morning, I walked into the pulpit, and you could see that Pastor Caldwell was wondering what in the world was going on. Then I announced it was Pastor's Appreciation Day, and we blessed him financially by receiving a special offering. Also, we had people come up and share what the Caldwells had meant to them.

Each year since, we have done this to let the pastor and his wife know that we love and appreciate them. However, several years ago, someone came to me who felt we were lifting up a man and not exalting Jesus. I searched my heart and the Bible and found 1 Timothy 5:17,18:

> **Let the elders that rule well be counted worthy of double honour, especially they who labour in the word and doctrine.**
>
> **For the scripture saith, Thou shalt not muzzle the ox that treadeth out the corn. And, The labourer is worthy of his reward.**

When I realized that the Bible said pastors are worthy of double honor, I realized we were on target. Pastors have authority and must give an account of that authority. They deserve appreciation. Hebrews 13:17 says:

**Obey them that have the rule over you, and submit yourselves: for they watch for your souls, as they that must give account, that they may do it with joy, and not with grief: for this is unprofitable for you.**

I want to challenge every staff member and every church member who reads this book to get together with others in your church and set aside a day to show your pastors that you love them. Pray and ask the Lord what He would have you do, and then bless them with the best you can. Do this once a year to encourage them. You will find that God will honor this, and the love of God will flow in your church.

### 4. *The family*

Paul wrote in Ephesians 6:1 for children to obey their parents in the Lord, *for this is right*. As long as you are living under the roof of your parents, you must submit to them. If you are over forty years old and still living with your mom and dad, then you will have to submit to them in many areas of your life. My suggestion is to move out. Once you are not living in their house, you are no longer under their authority. However, remember that the Bible says you are always to honor them.

### 5. *Employers*

Peter wrote that servants should be subject to their masters and not only to those masters who are "good and gentle." (1 Pet. 2:18.) That makes it very clear that we must submit on our jobs to whoever is in authority over us. That means to pray for your boss, and if they are harsh or demanding, pray that God will get hold of them and turn them into "gentle masters."

Stop complaining and start praying. Then make sure you are on time and do a good job. They will be ministered to by your diligence. If you do this, God will more than likely open a door for you to share Christ with them.

The centurion who told Jesus to just "speak the word" and his servant would be healed understood authority. The centurion was a man *in* authority. He also was a man *under* authority. Jesus said He had not found anyone in Israel with this kind of faith. Why did that Roman centurion have such faith? He *understood* authority. (Matt. 8:9.) He could tell that demons and disease were subject to the authority of Jesus.

In conclusion: *Authority is here to stay*. We will never graduate from under authority. When we get to heaven, we will still submit to authority. Those who climb God's ladder into spiritual authority and do exploits for Him are the ones who know how to submit and flow with authority. God will never exalt you into a greater place of authority until you learn how to submit to authority.

## Reproof of Instruction Is the Way of Life

The last key to maintaining a good attitude is *being big enough to be rebuked and corrected*. Proverbs 6:23 says that "reproofs of instruction" are the way of life. We will be reproved and corrected in life, because we are human and make mistakes. If you want to mature, you must remain teachable.

> **Reprove not a scorner, lest he hate thee: *rebuke* a wise man, and he will love thee.**
>
> **Give *instruction* to a wise man, and he will be yet wiser: *teach* a just man, and he will increase in learning.**
> **Proverbs 9:8,9**

If you are one who is going to rebuke, then be wise enough to *instruct* and *teach*. I have seen people who felt called to "rebuke," but there was no teaching or instruction.

That kind of rebuke amounts to criticism and results in nothing but wounds and strife. God never assigned anyone to break a person's spirit. We are always to rebuke with meekness and love and take the time to teach the person how to do right and what they have done wrong.

On the other hand, if you are the one being rebuked, do not get your feelings hurt. Be big enough to take it and go on without holding a grudge and being defensive. It is very clear from the Word of God that a wise man will listen to correction, and judge himself. (Prov. 13:1.) A fool despises any instruction.

> **The way of a fool is right in his own eyes: but he that hearkeneth unto counsel is wise.**
>
> **Proverbs 12:15**
>
> **He that refuseth instruction despiseth his own soul: but he that heareth reproof getteth understanding.**
>
> **Proverbs 5,10,32**
>
> **Smite a scorner, and the simple will beware: and reprove one that hath understanding, and he will understand knowledge.**
>
> **Proverbs 19:25**

I must admit that I have met some fools in my life. They will not take any correction. Their shortcomings and problems were always someone else's fault. They are always right. What do you do with people like that? You stay away from them and watch what happens to them. They will never fulfill God's will, because they will not admit mistakes.

We are told in the Bible to judge ourselves and make corrections when we need to change. If you refuse to judge yourself, you will face judgment on the sin in which you live.

I believe it is very important today to have people around us to whom we are accountable, people who can speak into our lives. That is why the Bible says to submit to

God-called leadership, so they can help us if we begin to miss it. We cannot afford to miss the will of God in our lives.

Stay humble before the Lord, and when you are corrected or rebuked, receive it and learn from it. Then you will grow into the place God intends for you to be. There is no growth without some pruning. God wants fruit to come forth in your life and remain.

# 5

# Keys to Teamwork

I want to begin this chapter with something the Holy Spirit quickened to me, and that is an analogy between an NFL football team and the operation of the local church.

**People involved and points to remember**

I. **Coaches in the press box.** They see the overall field, and they see the way the defense is set up. They can tell by this which play is the best to call, and they are the ones who call the plays. Their job is to watch the defense to spot any weakness, then quickly call a play to take advantage of it.

This is the **Father and the Son of God,** Who sit in the press box and call the plays. They know the devil's tactics and defenses and which play will work against them. Paul wrote that we should not let Satan take advantage of us, for we are not ignorant of his devices. (2 Cor. 2:11.)

There are three heavens in the universe. (2 Cor. 12:2.) The first heaven is over the earth where we live, the second is the realm where Satan, demons, and angels dwell, and the third heaven is where God's throne is. The Bible makes it clear that Satan is the prince and power of the air. God looks down on the second heaven and sees clearly the defense of the devil against the church.

He then calls down to the Coach on the playing field and communicates to him what the devil is doing, so he can then let the quarterback know what play to run.

The coaches in the press box will always make a video tape of every play, so they can take a look at the last play while another play is being run on the field. That way they can analyze the defense and see what the opposing team is setting up. Our Father has the ability to see past, present, and future. He knows the right play to call every time. It is up to us to listen to the **Coach on the field of play**.

II. **The coach on the field.** He assists in calling the plays, but his most important job is to communicate those plays to the quarterback. He is there to encourage and strengthen the team's confidence. He never leaves the field until the game is over.

The Coach on the field for the Church, of course, is the **Holy Spirit**. He is the Head Coach on the field of play with us. (John 16:7.) He is always encouraging us when we get tired or hurt. He will be with us until the game is over.

When a player is discouraged with his performance, the Coach begins to build up his confidence. He will tell that player that he *is* going to make it, he can win this game. That is the Word of the Holy Spirit to us. We can make it, we can win, we are the Lord's very best, and nothing is impossible with God on our side.

The Holy Spirit will only speak or call the plays that he hears from the Father. (John 16:13.) Then He communicates those directions to the quarterback.

III. **The Quarterback.** He is the head communicator on the playing field. He must effectively call the plays given to him by the coaches. He must run the offense. He depends fully on the coaches to spot the weaknesses in the defense in order to win the game. The quarterback must be healthy and strong in order to win the game. No team can win without a good quarterback.

This is the **Pastor**. He must call the play for the team. He must depend on the Holy Spirit to give orders and follow His instructions. Running the right play and gaining yards will come by being obedient to the Head Coach, the Holy Spirit.

As any head coach runs his team a little different from any other, so will the Holy Spirit run each local church in a different way. What works for one will not always work for another.

The Holy Spirit wants the pastor to hear the plays from Him. After the pastor has received the play, he must effectively communicate it to the team in order for the play to work. Many plays have failed and penalties resulted, because the players did not know the play or on what count the ball was to be snapped.

Pastors must also hand the ball off to the other "backs," so that their abilities and talents can be used in gaining yards for the team. Any quarterback understands the gifts and talents that are there to assist the team.

In our analogy, the "football" is the vision, and it must be handed to the other staff ministers, so that they can "make yardage." If a pastor hangs onto the vision because of insecurity, he will hinder the team. No quarterback can win the game by himself.

In fact, if a head coach sees a quarterback refusing to hand off or throw the football to another player, he will discipline him and take him out of the game if he does not make the adjustments. The most valuable person on the team is the quarterback, who controls the offense. But the quarterback knows his success depends fully upon those around him.

**Points to remember:**

A. No quarterback can win the game by himself. The other players must do their jobs in order to gain yards. Quarterbacks have been frustrated, bruised, hurt, and even knocked out of the game due to a lineman who let his defensive man through the line. Each player must do his job in order for the team to win.

B. The quarterback cannot do the job of a tackle just as a tackle cannot do the job of a quarterback. Each is gifted in his place. All must carry the same vision, and that is to score and to win the game.

C. Every quarterback must take time for a huddle. In the huddle, he calls the plays so each person knows his assignment for that down.

III. **Halfbacks, Fullbacks, and Ends.** They, along with the quarterback, must advance the ball. They must be strong, quick, and creative in making the right moves. They must not be concerned about which back is making the most yards. If one is having a good game, then *give him the ball*. The goal is to win the game, and not be concerned with who is scoring. These players, like the quarterback, will receive the majority of the recognition due to their special gifts and talents.

Once they receive the ball, it is up to them to think quickly and creatively in order to move it down the field. They depend on the linemen to clear the way for them. The first thing they must do is take the ball from the quarterback. Fumbles are caused by not remembering the basics.

These are the **Associate Ministers**. They are gifted by God to run with the vision and effectively communicate it to the people. They have the freedom to think creatively, but must remember to listen to the play the pastor calls, then take the hand off.

No halfback or fullback will call the play; it is always the quarterback. The different backs have the right to tell the quarterback that they are open, or that they know they can break through the line. But it is still up to the quarterback to call the play.

If the associates take the hand off from the pastor, then run in an opposite direction of the play, there will be major problems. They must go in the direction of the team. Just as a quarterback will be set down by the head coach if he does not listen to the play, so will the associates be set down by their pastors and the Holy Spirit if they try to do their own thing.

Creativity comes once they are running with the ball (vision). They must realize that once they have scored, it was a team effort and not theirs alone. Many a football player has become lifted up in pride thinking he alone was the reason his team won. Associates depend on the office staff and those in the ministry of helps to clear obstacles out of the way in order for their gifts to have the opportunity to come forth. Gifted athletes are stopped on the scrimmage line when the linemen are unable to do their jobs.

IV. **The Linemen.** They are the backbone and work horses of the offense. Their jobs are to protect the quarterback and clear the way for the backs to make yardage. They must listen to every play called and for the snap count, even though they are tired or hurt. They must have a great tolerance for pain. Linemen do not get a lot of fanfare but have great joy when their team scores. They are always the toughest and strongest on the team and must be determined that no defensive lineman is going to get through. Their attitudes are that no one sacks our quarterback or catches our backs behind the line.

This is the equivalent of the **Office Staff and Ministry of Helps**. They are the backbone of a church. They must stay built up, have a winning attitude, and determination that no devil gets our pastor. They do not get most of the fanfare, but every pastor and associate knows they are nothing without these workers. Everyone shares in the victory.

They must listen carefully to the Pastor to know the direction in which the team is going. Joy comes from seeing souls born into the Kingdom because they did their jobs.

Teams win through unity, motivation for winning, determination, endurance, practice, and ability. These are all true in the ministry. When one scores, we all score. When one wins, the whole team wins. At the end of the Superbowl, all the players on the winning team receive rings and a big bonus check. No matter their position, each player receives the same prize. As we are faithful to our positions, we — like Superbowl champs — will receive from God the same reward because we did the job He called us to do and we won as a team.

I would like to discuss some keys to teamwork that are a must in fulfilling the vision of the local church.

## Keys to Teamwork

The first key is *walking without offense*. The main reason why people leave churches is because they get offended. Instead of dealing with whatever was said or done, they harbor bitterness from offenses in their hearts and end up leaving their churches.

There was a documentary on TV recently on how Africans catch monkeys. Now a monkey is very intelligent, so the African had to do something to out think the animal. He first put a cage on the ground with a bright object inside it. The door to the cage was left open to tempt the monkey to go in. When he did, a trap was set on the door to cause it to close and catch him. But the monkey would not go into the cage.

So the Africans closed the cage and made the wire around the cage just big enough so the monkey could get his hand in the cage. Now, when the monkey saw the bright object, he put his hand through the wire and grabbed it, but could not get it out of the cage. With the object in hand, he could not pull it through. He could only be free if he would let go of the object. The African then took a club and knocked the monkey over the head, and it died. Now, you would think that the monkey would have been smarter than that.

Many who are backslidden today are like these monkeys. They reached into the devil's "cage" by taking hold of an offense and refuse to let go. He is hitting them over the head with sickness, strife, and all types of marriage, family and financial problems. They have given themselves over to bitterness, and it is destroying them.

All they have to do to be free and remain free of that trap is to *let go* of hurts and wounds. God can heal and restore a person immediately if he will forgive offenses and repent of bitterness. Some readers have been hurt by their pastors or church leaders and allowed that to build up. If you are leaving your church or have already left, *please stop*! Go to the pastor or the one who offended you, and ask him to forgive you. That is the only way you are going to have true peace in your heart and family.

Anyone can take offense, get hurt, and walk out, but it takes a real man or woman of God to make it right. There is no Biblical reason to hold a grudge or to live in resentment. And there is every reason not to. Matthew 18:34,35 says:

> **And his lord was wroth, and delivered him to the tormentors, till he should pay all that was due him.**
>
> **So likewise shall my heavenly Father do also unto you, if ye from your hearts forgive not *every one* his brother their trespasses.**

The next key to teamwork is *using all your talents and abilities*. The church must function like a team, and in order to do so, the team needs your talents and abilities. I believe you have talents lying dormant just waiting to be used. In the midst of being faithful where you are placed, begin to draw on the abilities in you. You have the Creator on the inside. Pray and trust Him for His complete will to be fulfilled in your life.

In Matthew 25, we find the Parable of the Talents as told by Jesus. Matthew 25:13,14 says:

> **Watch therefore, for ye know neither the day nor the hour wherein the Son of man cometh.**
>
> **For the kingdom of heaven is as a man traveling into a far country, who called his own servants, and delivered them his goods.**

Jesus was comparing the Kingdom of God to a man taking a far journey and calling his servants together. Now this shows us Jesus as the one taking the journey, and He has called you and me together and delivered unto us His goods. So each of us has received something from Jesus.

Matthew 25:15 says:

> **And unto one he gave five talents, to another two, and to another one; to every man according to his several ability; and straight way took his journey.**

Jesus uses money as the example, but as you continue through Chapter 25, you find in verse 35 these words:

> **For I was an hungered, and ye gave me meat: I was thirsty and ye gave me drink.**

This proves to us that He was not only referring to money, but also to us using the gifts and callings we have to help others. So I am going to use the word *talents* to refer to our gifts and callings. Jesus gave to one five talents, and to another two talents, and to another one. He then took his journey after He was raised from the dead and now has given to each of us certain talents to be used for His Kingdom.

You may say, "Brother Nance, I don't have any gifts, or talents."

But you do, according to 1 Peter 4:10, which says that Jesus gave us gifts from God. We have no choice in the matter; Jesus is the one who gave out the talents. So if you

have two talents and someone else got five, it does no good to be jealous or complain.

God did not call me up before His throne before I was born and say to me, "Terry, I am now ready to allow you to be born in the earth, but before you go, which gifts would you like to take with you?"

I would say, "Well, Lord! Give me that Apostle gift and that Prophet gift, and while You're at it, throw in gifts of healing and working of miracles."

The bottom line is that each of us is only accountable for his own gifts and callings and not for someone else's. Matthew 25:19 tells us there will come a "reckoning day." Romans 14:10 says that we will all stand before the judgment seat of Christ.

I know personally I will not stand before God and give account to Him for the ability to play the drums. I cannot play the drums, because I have very little rhythm. So, if it is not there, then it is not there. But I do have other abilities that I can use to bless the Kingdom of God.

As you read verses 22 and 23, you find Jesus saying to the one who had received two talents the same thing he said to the first one to whom He gave the five talents. This proves to us that if we are faithful to do with what God has given us, we will all receive the same reward. God only holds you responsible for what He gave you. If I am faithful to do what God called me to do as a Senior Associate of Agape Church, and Pastor Caldwell is faithful to do what God calls him to do, then we will receive the same reward, because we were faithful with the gifts and callings we both received.

The Spirit of God is saying loud and clear that it is time for us to release our gifts. We do not want to be like the servant in the parable who received one talent and went and buried it. That man was called "a wicked and slothful" servant.

65

You are part of a team, and a chain is only as strong as its weakest link. So rise up and bind away fear and get rid of all hurt and offense and begin to do something for the Kingdom. God will begin to add gifts, as you release what you already have.

Do not be like the man who prayed, "God, use me! Use me!" then after working in the church for a while, he went back to the Lord and said, "Lord, I just feel used."

## God Does Not Create "Throw-Aways"

The next key to teamwork is a major one: *Know that you are important and needed*. God never created anything to be discarded. In the world's system, we place great value on the things that are one of a kind. These are the items that are priceless. You must understand that God made you one of a kind, and you are a priceless gift to the Church.

When you take a close look at 1 Corinthians 12:12-25, you will see the importance of each part of the body. The Apostle Paul made a comparison of the physical body to the Body of Christ, and pointed out that the body has many members but all work as a team.

This is how the Body of Christ and the local churches should function. As you read those verses in which Paul points out that the eye cannot do without the hand, and vice versa, we can see that he is saying there should be no jealousy between "parts" of the Body.

Our hands, feet, eyes are all important parts of the physical body. We would look very funny if we were just one great big nose. Thank God, we are not made like that. You are what God made you in the Body of Christ, and you are a vital part. The key is your hooking up with the other parts and working together toward a common goal.

And Paul wrote that it was God Who set the members in the Body as it pleased Him. God made each of us unique

and gave us qualities that no others possess exactly as we do. Every Christian has something valuable to God and to the Body. So, if I am called to function as a hand, then it is up to me to be the best hand that I can be. My gifts and talents please God, so I know that I am valuable to the team.

Paul pointed out that even the uncomely, or unseen, parts of the body are as important as the others. There is nothing beautiful about a liver, for example. But you must realize that you cannot live without one. I believe the inward, or uncomely, parts of the body represent the ministry of helps. They are always in the background working, but you do not see them that much.

I have heard teachers refer to those in the ministry of helps as being in a lower position or as "playing second fiddle" in the Body. That grieves my spirit, and I believe it also grieves the Holy Spirit. In their function, the ministry of helps are just as important to God as the five-fold ministry gifts.

A great evangelist told about dreaming of standing before the judgment seat of Christ. There on a table were all types of crowns, but in the middle was a huge crown decked out with jewels, by far the most beautiful of all.

He stood there and thought, "That must be my crown, for I have won millions to Christ."

Finally an angel called his name and picked up a small crown right next to the big one for him. The evangelist stopped the angel and asked if he knew who he was and that he had won millions to Jesus.

But the angel said, "Yes, but this is the right crown." He was sad and a little distraught over receiving a small crown.

Then a little elderly woman's name was called out, and she went up to have the large, beautiful crown placed on her head. So the evangelist immediately wanted to know

who she was, and the angel said, "This is the woman who faithfully prayed for you."

He received a revelation that God said more abundant honor sometimes is bestowed on those that we think to be less important (1 Cor. 12:22-24.)

If you are going to fulfill your part in the Body, you must stop looking at your inabilities and start using your abilities. Get connected with the other parts, be faithful to your local church, and begin to run with the vision of the church

## Run With the Vision

In Acts 4, we are told of the disciples being threatened for praying in Jesus' name. They got together with the brethren and began to pray, and when they had prayed, the house where they were was shaken. They were all filled with the Holy Spirit and spoke God's Word with boldness.

Acts 4:32 makes a very important point. The "multitude of them that believed" were all of *one heart and one soul*. In other words, they were in agreement. That is the key to seeing a great shaking of the Holy Spirit in our churches and cities. We are all of one heart when we are born again, because we all belong to Jesus. But are we all "one soul"?

A corporate anointing came on them, because they were in unity. They all had the same vision: to take the Gospel to the world no matter the personal cost. They were determined to flow together, recognize the authority of the apostles, and follow what Jesus was saying through them.

God speaks the vision into the heart of a local pastor, and that vision must get inside of the believers. Then they are to run in heart and soul toward the fulfillment of it. A corporate anointing on a local church will impact a city.

What is the vision of your local church? What is God saying through your pastor? Take hold of that vision and

begin to run with your pastor, heart and soul. It is the plan and will of God that you flow with your pastor's heart and soul. Paul prayed for the Corinthians to *all speak the same thing* and have no divisions among them. (1 Cor. 1:10.)

If you are trying to run with a vision that God has not given your pastor, then you are going to create division. You need to stop and hook into what God is saying to your pastor and begin running in the same direction.

Do you really want to do exploits for God? Are you willing to find your place in the Body and get connected with the other members of your local church? Are you ready to release the gifts and talents God has put in you? If so, begin by becoming involved. God will never force Himself on you. He gives you the right to choose. But think what can be accomplished for God's Kingdom when you begin to do your part.

We are called to be armorbearers one for another. That commitment is a lifetime responsibility. Now is the time to pick up your spiritual sword and join the ranks of God's great army. We will stand victorious together because where one will put a thousand to flight, two will put ten thousand to flight.

The last and final key to teamwork is to *rest in God, and let Him lead you into the perfect plan for your life.* You must learn to trust God and let Him bring to pass the course laid out in His mind for you. We should not lean to our own understanding. (Prov. 3:5,6.) God is the one who directs our paths.

While attending Rhema in 1979, the Lord instructed us to resign from a church where we were working and just attend another one. Then, for the first time in my life, I was faced with no requirements to be at church. However, Kim and I made sure we were there three or four times a week.

I went to work part time at a shoe store, and Kim worked as a private sitter for elderly people in a nursing home.

Every day for seven or eight months, I went to work ten minutes early to sit in the car and speak out these words:

"I have a call on my life, and I am not going to sell shoes and smell feet for the rest of my life. When I get out of this car, Lord, I thank you that I am walking into the ministry where I am working fulltime."

We believed God in every area of our lives, especially in the financial area. Kim would tell the old people she took care of about Jesus. They would get saved, but because they were so old, they would die. As long as they were alive, Kim got paid. When they died, she had no job!

I went over to the nursing home and declared to them, "You will live and not die" — but they died anyway. I asked Kim why she always got the hopeless cases to look after. Why didn't they assign her someone who had some life in them?

Three weeks before school was out that year, another lady Kim was helping died. Then my boss came in and said the shoe business was being taken over in three weeks by his son, and he did not need me. There we were with neither of us having jobs and no prospect of joining a church staff.

All the churches we contacted wanted to know was whether my wife played the piano and sang. Well, she sang, but could not play the piano, so they would say, "Sorry. We need someone with talent."

I began to think, "Dear Lord, I could be the biggest jerk around and I could be a thief, but if my wife could play the piano, I could make it in the ministry!"

I was so down one night that I lay on the floor of our apartment and cried my eyes out. I had the biggest "pity party" I had ever had. In the middle of this, suddenly Jesus interrupted my party. His voice was so clear.

He said, "Son, why are you crying? Don't you realize I am up here interceding for you?"

That shook me to my toes. I jumped up and began to shout and dance and praise God for His mercy. I did not know how He would do it, but I was then sure that He did have a plan for my life.

The next Sunday morning at church, a young man came up to me whom I had never met. He had met my mother and seen a picture of me when he visited my parents' church in Arkansas. He was not looking for me, but that morning he just "happened" to sit a few seats away from me and recognized me. He asked me to lunch.

Three weeks later, we graduated from Rhema and decided to move back to my home town of Magnolia, Arkansas, where I could work in my brother's shoe store. When we arrived at my parents' home, however, my brother said he could not use me. Things were not getting any better fast.

Before leaving Tulsa, we had received one invitation to hold a small seminar in Florida. Right before we were to leave, the young man who had introduced himself to us at church in Tulsa called and told us about Pastor Happy Caldwell. He had just started a church in Little Rock and was looking for some people to help him. The young man asked if I would be interested in meeting with Pastor Caldwell. Needless to say, I did not need to look at my ministry calendar, because I did not have one.

So after we got back from Florida, we went to Little Rock. There were many other divine connections that God brought about along the way to get my wife and me hooked up with the Caldwells to help them with their vision of reaching Little Rock for Jesus.

You see, God is the best "chess player" there ever will be. He knows how to put you where He wants you. You may find yourself some place and not understand why, but if you trust God, you will see in the end that He was working out His divine plan.

In this book, I have shared some of the many challenges in my life as examples of those that will come when you are in the will of God. But He has delivered us out of them all. He orchestrated events in our lives to plant us where He wanted. It has been here that God has caused us to *Bloom Where We Have Been Planted.*

Many are called, but few are chosen. Stepping into that place of the chosen of God comes by prayer, faith, integrity, diligence, and excellence of ministry. You must determine to have those in your life and be committed to the will of God no matter the cost.

All of us are God's armorbearers, marching forward to serve in this earth, to do our parts in evangelizing the nations. Let us not be weak in faith and wander in our callings any longer. Let us do what our hands find to do, serve our God-called leaders, and pray in the last-day move of the Holy Spirit.

This is *our* generation, *our* day and hour, and *our* time to rise up and be the lights God wants us to be. We are God's army, God's voice, God's instrument in the earth: *We are the Local Churches.*

To contact the author, write:

Terry Nance
Agape Church
P. O. Box 22007
Little Rock, Arkansas 72221-2007

*Please include your prayer
requests and comments
when you write.*

Additional copies of
this book and
*God's Armorbearer, I*
are available from
your local bookstore.



In Canada contact:
Word Alive
P. O. Box 670
Niverville, Manitoba
Canada ROA 1EO

## The Harrison House Vision

Proclaiming the truth and the power
Of the Gospel of Jesus Christ
With Excellence;

Challenging Christians to
Live victoriously,
Grow spiritually,
Know God intimately.